Copyright 2014 Cricket Cottage Publishing. All rights reserved, Printed in the United States of America. Excerpts as permitted under the United States Act of 1976, no part of the publication may be reproduced or distributed in any form or by any means, or stored in a database or retrieval system, without the prior written permission of the publisher.

For information about group sales and permission, contact Cricket Cottage Publishing, LLC, 4409 Hoffner Avenue, Suite 127, Orlando, Florida 32812 or call 407-255-7785.

Illustrations by: Ron L. Clowney

ISBN: 978-0-692-02401-0
ISBN-10: 0692024018

Dedication and Acknowledgements

This work is dedicated to the favorable future, of the children, youth, and adults who have the opportunity to work with the material herein, and those with whom they interact. It is also dedicated to the hope for uplifting solutions to human problems, and to the fruition of a more reasonable, more productive, and less violent society. Finally, it is dedicated to the unfolding of an abundance of civility, liberty, love and good will.

It is also important to acknowledge that this production could not have come about without help from a great team of people around me (which are too many to name), inspiring me, supporting me, preparing a way for me, and loving me. This includes first all my ancestors, especially my parents Edward and Melma Murray, my siblings, Veronica Koscik, Jackie White and Michael Murray, and my wife and son Lorraine and Shiloh Murray, my various teachers and instructors throughout my life, my many encouraging and supportive colleagues, my many patients and clients from whom I also learned, and my many, many loving friends. Thanks to my administrative assistants who've helped in the presentation of the work to schools thus far to include Ms. JoAnn Osborn, Mr. Larry Byrd, and Ms. Margo Bennette-Cole. Clearly, the staff and owner(s) of Cricket Cottage Publishing Company were also pivotal (here a special thanks to Mr. John Hurst who helped with the reprinting), and let me extend a special thanks to all those who, at some future point, chose to assist in the propagation of this important work. Again, thank you all.

TABLE OF CONTENTS

	PAGE
Introduction and Prospectus	I-II
Careful Serious Raps About **"When Push Comes To Shove"**	III
Introduction Of The Three Lead Characters	1
Description Of Fast And Furious Characters	2
Description Of Careful Serious Character	3
Description Of So Mysterious Character	4
Description Of Leadership Role Of Characters	5
The Change Page-Valley Try Drought Page	6
The Decision Meeting Of The Three Leaders.	7
Each Leaders' Thoughts On The Unknown	8
Each Leader's Separate Decision On What To Do	9
Fast And Furious' Decision To Leave With His Herd	10
So Mysterious' Decision To Stay	11
The Consultation Page-Careful Serious Consults An Elder	12
The Overcome Obstacles With Hard Work Faith And Courage Page	13
The Attainment Of An Intermediate Goal Page	14
Careful Serious Confronts "The Sage Of Trees"	15
The Birds Give The Directions To The "Alternative" Valley Page	16
The Birds Give Warnings of Dangers In The "Alternative" Valley Page	17
The Birds Give Final Directions To The "Alternative" Valley Page	18
The Careful Serious Takes Notes On The Directions Page	19
The Fast & Furious Herd Gets Captured By Ogres Page	20
The Fast & Furious Discovers Some of His Crew were Captured By Ogres Page	21
The Ores Enslave Some of The Fast & Furious Crew Page	22
The Fast & Furious Tries To Cope With The Traumatic Loss of Some Of His Crew Page	23
The Fast & Furious Employs The "Quick Movement" Strategy To Deal With Dangers Page	24
The Fast & Furious Crew Find Luscious Lake Page	25
The Fast & Furious Crew Gorge Themselves On Food At Luscious Lake Page	26
The Wolves Launch A Sneak Attack On The Fast & Furious Crew Page	27
The Fast & Furious And Spouse Flee, Escape, And Survive The Attack Page	28
The Fast & Furious And Spouse Hide From The Wolves Page	29
The Careful Serious Tries To Convince So Mysterious To Leave With His Crew Page	30

	PAGE
The So Mysterious Refuses To Leave Page	31
The Careful Serious Crew Departs The Valley Try Page	32
The So Mysterious Gives His Final Speech To His Crew Page	33
The So Mysterious Crew Is "Wiped Out" Page	34
The Careful Serious Crew Successfully Traverses The Ogre's Danger Page	35
The Careful Serious Crew Successfully Traverses The Luscious Lake Danger Page	36
The Careful Serious Crew Finds Fast & Furious And Spouse Page	37
The Careful Serious Crew With Fast & Furious And Spouse Find The Wall of Stones Page	38
The Combined Crew Reach Their Objective In Valley Alternative Page	39
The Post Story Assignment Pages	40-49
Teaching/Learning Format 1 Page	50
Teaching/Learning Format 2 Page	51
367 High Schools Student Ratings of When Push Comes To Shove	52-54
Thematic Table of Contents	55-63
Self-Worth Diagram in Reference To Threats To The Survival of The Ego	64
An Example Of One Young Person's Narrative About The Work	65
Recommendations on When Push Comes To Shove	66-70
Congressional Award From The Congress of The United States of America	71
Newspaper Article On The Book	72-73
About The Author	74

Introduction And Prospectus On *When Push Comes to Shove: A Tale of Three Goats Lives*
A Story-Based Critical Thinking Training Program To Enhance
Critical Thinking, Reading, Speech Memory and Vocabulary Skills

I. SUMMARY

This work presents a highly engaging and picturesque pedagogical story that serves as a foundation for critical thinking training. It is also a tool to enhance cognitive development in reading skills, logical and sequential thinking, speech, and memory and vocabulary skills. In addition, the work helps to infuse participants with a *facility* for many of idioms and sayings that are at the crux of crucial language and communication skills, important in western society-so it can also be used as a basis to teach English comprehension from a foreign language (*esp.* with the DVD version). The entire story is told in rhyme. While very entertaining as a presentation, the work's greatest merit may lie in the application of the it's training programs. Its *target population* spans youth from ages 8-25 (*esp.* with the DVD version). Programs are aimed at advancing abilities in the areas cited above and are adaptable to virtually all levels of ability from preteens to young adults, from slow to advanced learners. In addition, it also has relevance and lessons for adults and particularly the *business world*. The story is essentially about *adaptation to change (or crises)*. It captures how certain *predisposed* response-styles tend to *play out* when one is confronted by *crises level* change. While *crisis level change*, encompasses many commonly acknowledged experiences in society (e.g. grief, great personal loss, etc.) It is also very *subjective* in nature depending to a great extent upon how the individual *translates* his or her experience. Nevertheless, this work offers solidly grounded *coping guidelines*, and does so in a way that its' messages can easily *adhere* to one's *psyche* for a lifetime.

Theme: The story outlines of the fate of the three major characters, three goats, whom each are leaders of their own herd of goats. As their names imply, each of the goats has a distinct character and manner (which is emulated by the rest of their herd) that guides their approach to dealing with change or problems.

(1) SO MYSTERIOUS	(2) CAREFUL-SERIOUS	(3) FAST-&-FURIOUS

ABOUT THE CAST

SO MYSTERIOUS: This individual has a character which is somewhat timid in nature. He does not take well to moving in new directions, and tends to hold steadfast to his belief in the status quo or tried and true methods of solving problems. He is *unlikely* to venture out of his *comfort zone*.

FAST-&-FURIOUS: This character is indulgent and impulsive in nature. He has very little 0, is extremely adventurous and always in a rush to do things.

CAREFUL-SERIOUS: This individual represents somewhat of a balance between the previous two, however, the cornerstone of his character is that he expands the scope of his *response-options* through consultation, research, study, and reflection.

Story Dilemma: In the beginning of the story, the various dispositions of the characters are rather benign. However, as their conditions and circumstances *suddenly change* (i.e. drought of the *Valley Try* in which they live), so do the *consequences* for how each of the characters approaches the situation. The advantages and pitfalls of each problem-solving method are revealed as the story unfolds.

Sample of Lesson Plan: Students can work in pairs. A *reader* student in the pair reads each page 1 at a time. After each page reading, the *reader* student then ask the *listening student* to describe as much as they can recall of what has just been read to them. The *reader* student (or someone else) then rates the *listening student's* recall on a scale of 1, 2, or 3. Students obtain a maximum score of 3 points for what they recall from each page. Students then switch places. Student's total scores are obtained by summing up the scores for each page. Many other learning formats and exercises are also included in the work.

II. MARKET

Most Children's Books, are of the "Dr. Seuss" variety, appealing to the very young audience with very simplistic notions about ideas that have fairly limited relevance to the real issues that confront us as we broach the many awesome tasks that growth and development entails throughout our lives. **When Push Comes To Shove: A Tale of Three Goats Lives** appeals to a somewhat older youth audience, a group whose developmental needs are *largely ignored* by the current configuration of the literary market.

Teachers, and school counselors, particularly, will find this material of immeasurable value. This inasmuch as the work allows for the teaching of adaptive ideas and principles in a somewhat surreptitious manner, offering an avenue for circumventing emotional defenses (particularly prevalent when working with older youths (who may often be in a rather oppositional phase of development). Along with the story and DVD, ancillary materials are presented that can be used as a springboard for addressing numerous concerns faced by today's youth. That work can serve as the ***mainstay*** for inculcating values and habits critical to survival and prosperity in modern society.

Already, at this early juncture, limited field testing has evidenced *strikingly* positive results. Wider adoption by even one school or district would almost certainly improve and even save a great many lives. With an ever-increasing need for addressing the topics *at the heart* of this production, young people, schools, and society at large are currently *ripe and ready* for such a work.

III. CROSSOVER APPLICATIONS

The characters and structure of this work makes it highly amenable to broad range of formats (i.e. movies, video games, plays, cartoons, etc).

IV. ABOUT THE AUTHOR

The author, Dr. Edward L. Murray III, practiced clinical psychology in a private practice in San Diego, California for over two decades. **When Push Comes to Shove: A Tale of Three Goats Lives** emerged as part of a package promoting positive mental health and education. Its metaphorical approach to intervention can often be effective where other methods might fail. It has been *well-received and effective* across a wide range of cultural groups. Dr. Murray continues a long-standing family tradition of service and education. His *grandfather*, Edward L. Murray Sr., was, as far as we know, the *first* African American principle of a public school in Baltimore, Maryland (and he was highly regarded for the ability of *"total recall"*). His *father* was the first African American *finance officer* to serve in the U.S. Army. Dr. Murray was born in Ft. Meade, Maryland, is the son of a career military officer and his wife, Edward and Melma Murray (an accomplished artist). He is the second eldest of four siblings, two sisters and one brother (all very accomplished in their own right). He was reared in a variety of cultural and geographic settings. This contributed to an ability to develop culturally universal methods of interacting with others. The use of stories, metaphor and symbols thus became a major feature of his interaction style. Dr. Murray received his undergraduate psychology degree from Indiana University in Bloomington, Indiana and his master's and doctorate degrees in clinical psychology from Arizona State University. After completing an internship at the Salt Lake City, VA Medical Center, he worked on a Native American Indian reservation in Parker, Arizona, with the Colorado River Indian Tribes, for approximately one year before beginning in private practice in San Diego, California. He was active *lifelong* in the martial art of Judo (has at least three gold medals as collegiate national champion), plays chess, writes music, plays the piano, the guitar, the harmonica and is an avid singer.

Careful Serious Raps About *When Push Comes To Shove*

"Just know these words are utensils,
to unleash our potential
'cuz we can't come second-rate
when we were born to be great
won't let ya fall in the *abyss*
'Naw naw' we coming with *this*
that's right we're here to wreak havoc
on the norms they've established
'cuz on all that shucking and jiving,
and that back room conniving…
we're 'gonna shine a big light
on what's wrong and what's right,
so come on people *hold tight*
'cuz we are in for a *fight*
we've 'gotta make us unite
so we don't suffer plight
and go through pain, *misery*
that *never* had to be."

"We hope to make a revision,
on how we go through decisions
so we can work it all out
not getting *lost* in our doubts
on how it is we proceed
when caught up in high weeds,
so then we' make our way through
and we know just how to do…
to come up on our situation
and then lift up our station
'cuz it's our dedication
to bring on our elevation
with this mighty righteous adjunct
to a good education…
now let us fan it all out
across all the great nations"

A tale is told, of Three Goats live's,
Three goats who lived in the, Valley Try.
Their views of life most curious. . .
Each goat a different theorist . . .

Goat one, named " Fast-&-Furious",
Goat two, called "Careful-Serious"
& Goat three, named "So-Mysterious",
Were all, indeed, quite curious!

The names they had, were true to fact.
They got these names for how they'd act.

Fast-&-Furious moved with haste,
To do things quickly was his taste.
He'd say "Let's get it going & move with speed,
In taking care of all our needs".
He played, and worked, and even ate!
As though he had, no time to wait

Careful-Serious made his mark
By taking care to learn each part,
Of all the things that came his way.
He studied them, and then he'd say:
"Let's check it out and think it through"
"And then we'll know just what to do"

Of **So-Mysterious** it was said
"Just Chillin'" was what's in his head
And keeping clear of any shock.
Was said to be his trade & stock
Caution was his major sign.
In all he did, he took his time.
He also was quite prone to scare,
And never would he take a dare.

Each goat grew up to lead a herd,
That followed by their guiding words.
That is, to say they took their cue
To act the way their leaders do.

Now though each herd had different strokes,
They somehow found a way to cope.
Cause in the great fair Valley Try,
Abundance bloomed and all was nigh.

There was plenty to drink and eat
And never was there too much heat,
Nor did it ever get too cold
So gardens filled and fruits shone bold.

But then... it came, misfortune struck!
The Valley Try... was drying up!
The sunshine shone relentlessly!

It was a striking sight to see.
Fields of green, soon turned to brown
And fruits, were no where to be found.

Soon it came, the three goats tried
To figure out how they'd get by!
They met and talked and tried to plan
On this dilemma, where should they stand?

They'd heard stories about a land
Where flowing rivers were at hand.
But also, it was said that there...
Were perils, that would curl your hair!
This Valley, named Alternative
Had fearsome beast, which in it lived!
Of course, each goat had different views,
On what it was, that they should do!

Fast-&-Furious said "lets move"!!!
My hunger I must quickly soothe!

So-Mysterious said, "let's wait!
Time will change our Valley's fate.
Careful-Serious said let's give,
Some thought to land Alternative.
Well... they could not come to agree,
On how it was, they should proceed.
So, each goat took charge their separate herds
Whom followed each goat's guiding words

Fast-&-Furious said "move-out!!!"
His herd charged on. with cheers and shouts.
To questions on the danger there...
He'd say, "we do not really care".
You see, we do not easily fear,
And our chance is better there than here.

So mysterious said, "we'll stay"!
And time will make a better way".
For us this seems the better stance
That to remain is our best chance.
Our ways here are quite tried and true
And this we know just how to do.

Careful-Serious asked around
To learn if stories told were sound.
A wise old goat said he should see
"The Talking Oak".. "The-Sage-Of-Trees."
The Sage-Of-Trees, it was professed!
Had knowledge, more than all the rest.

But, this Sage-Of-Trees, lived on a hill,
Whose climb, was quite a "bitter pill".
In fact, it was a mountain peak!

A place not meant, for those who are meek.
In places it grew very steep!
Ascent was truly quite a feat.

Cause winds blow quite incessantly,
It's cloudy, cold there, constantly.
Still... Careful-Serious moved ahead,
Kept in his heart, what old goat said.
But... this effort, surely had him pressed,
And often, put him to a test.

Still step-by-step, he made his climb!.
At last... he saw the tell-tail sign.
Branches reaching for the sky!
While at its base, two holes like eyes....

As Careful-Serious neared great oaks' floor,
The howling winds became no more!
The air warmed and then all around,
Were singing birds, with pretty sounds.

"Great Sage-Of-Trees" he did begin,
"Hush-hush" it's leaves retorted then.

He sat, and quietly... obeyed,

Then heard the bird's lyrics to say:
"You seek now to unfold a plan,
To travel to a distant land.
The Valley-of-Alternative
Is where you seek a place to live.
Though there it's true abundance thrives,
One must take care to stay alive.

Cross Valley Try and to the West.
To go at crack of dawn is best.
As you leave the Valley Try
You'll see a stone shape like a Y.
That's sitting rather upside-down
Go through the middle not around.

Walking straight in that direction
Will keep your herd in good protection.
Then you will see the forest door,
And just inside a corridor.
Follow this path until you hear
A waterfall then left you'll steer.

You'll come upon a luscious lake,
With fruits there that are yours to take.
Feed when the sun is at it's best,
Before the sun sets down to rest.
Take what you need but do not tarry
Or meet there with a fate quite scary.

Then go back the way you came,
　Back to the corridor again.
Turn your herd then to the right
And there you see just out of sight,
A wall of stones shaped like a heart
　And at its base, a covered part,

　　　　Go through the weeds you'll see a door
　　　　Go through and you'll find even more.
　　　　　A clearing and a gentle place
　　　　　With lots of land and open space."

Careful-Serious took notes,
Then left to tell his herd of goats.
Strange, but on the trip back home
The winds were still and sunshine shone.

Meanwhile
Herd Fast-&-Furious had found,
The "Y", that was sitting upside-down.
On either side, his herd was sent,
Though some right through the middle went.
All those who went on either side
Met Ogres towering in size.
The Ogres grabbed all goats they saw,
Scooped them up, their horns and all.
They put the goats inside a sack
Then flung them 'cross their massive backs

Now those that through the Y had wondered,
Escaped the ogre's fearsome plunder.
They saw their numbers had grown thin,
Turned round to see the ogres' sin.
They stood and stared their mouths agape
As not a single goat escaped.
Who did not walk inside the Y
That upon its' head did lie.

The Ogres took them to a cave
And told them there they'd work as slaves
The Ogres strapped, them to a wheel
On which they ground the Ogres meal
They ground their bread from day to night
It was a hard and wretched plight
And at the morning of each day,
The Ogres drained their milk away!

Now, Fast-&-Furious was in the group
Of goats who formed the remaining troop.
He walked ahead with naught to say
And found the forest entryway.

When just inside the forest door
As they reached the corridor.
He thought of what had just took place,
Then, trying to lead his herd with grace,
He said "We must speed-up our pace
I think this can improve our case.

This Valley named Alternative
Is not an easy place to live!
There are things that in the shadows lurk!
But I've a plan that just might work.
If we keep us moving fast,
Perhaps this tact will help us last."

So they pick-up in their stride
Hoping, this would turn the tide.
Moved quickly across the forest floor,
But some strayed from the corridor!
All those, who from this path, did stray
Soon found, that they had lost their way.

They searched, but were lost for all their days,
Cause the forest here twists like a maze...
Herd Fast-&-Furious numbered now just nine!
But Luscious Lake, they chanced to find.
They stood in awe what they did see...
Sweet fruits, and milk, and honey trees!
Sparkling water flowing down
And vegetables that did abound.

Fast-&-Furious charged ahead
His herd then followed in his stead.
On moist and succulent delights
They reveled, in their every bite.
They ate till day had turned to night
And did not see just out of sight.

Piercing eyes had gathered round.
Had moved in close without a sound...
Then, with stunning speed and grace,
They pounced, and showed the herd their face....
The Wolves, of Valley of Alternative,
Had found a meal on which to live!

With growls, and snarls and striking size,
They caught the herd quite by surprise.
With exception of just two,
The herd of goats they did undo.
These goats, which managed to escape,
Were those who'd kept themselves awake.
And when the wolves made their attack,
They were not lying on their back.
And the speed for which their herd was known,
Had kept their fate from being sown.

They ran back toward the corridor
And hid along the forest floor.
They cried, as it was very clear
That just they two had made it here...
Fast-&-Furious and his mate,
The only two, who now were safe.

Meanwhile,
back at Valley Try,
Herd Careful-Serious lingered nigh.
Waiting till the crack of dawn,
To begin their venture on.
"So mysterious" they did implore,
Won't you think this through once more?
Although we love the Valley Try,
I think it's clear we said good-bye!

Things here have gotten out of hand,
Our fields of plenty now are sand.
Our river water is but a trickle!
This is no time for being fickle."
There's been a change in our condition
And we must be about our mission
Now that push has come to shove
We must preserve the life we love
And act to move decisively
And find a better place to be.

But So-Mysterious did reply,
"To Valley Try my heart is tied!
Besides, we know not what awaits!
In lands of strange, uncertain fates.
I'm not the kind to take the risk!
On what could go wrong I've made a list.
Come and read it you will see!
Valley Try's where we should be."

Careful-Serious said "okay!!!",
I see you're one, who won't be swayed!
Still let the youngest two within your herd
leave with our herd, please hear these words!
Now comes the light of early day!
It's time... we must be on our way."
They gathered all that they could bring!
Supplies, and sentimental things.
And in the mornings' early light,
Herd Careful-Serious, walked out of sight!
Across Valley Try, and to the West...
And the Careful-Serious herd had left.

So-Mysterious was dismayed,
That Careful-Serious hadn't stayed.
But two from his herd he did let leave
As Careful Serious did with him plead
Then... he gave his herd a winded speech,
In which he tried his best to reach.
All in his large and loyal herd,
With what turned out were fatal words.

"We'll never leave the Valley Try.
It's to this land our souls are tied.
Though times are hard we'll see it through,
This path we must believe is true.
I know that in tomorrow's light
We'll see the end, of this fateful plight."

Herd So-Mysterious settled in.
But over time, they did grow thin...
Cause rain forgot the Valley Try
And searing heat was ever nigh.
Herd So-Mysterious soon grew weak,
At last, they hadn't strength... to speak.
Then, with the passing of the days,
All turned to dust... and blew away!

Meanwhile,
herd Careful-Serious had moved along
The path laid out in lyric song
When he had seen the Sage-of-Trees
Its birds have given him the key
To cross Valley Alternative
And find a better place to live
They followed in the path explained.
And herd Careful-serious was maintained
Throughout their long and trying trip
All the herd stayed firm and fit

Then when they reached the luscious lake
Not till the scheduled time did they take
Their fill of fruits and milk and honey,
Their hearts were bright, their souls were sunny
Then, just as it was so explained
They did not tarry, none remained.

Then, as they reached the corridor
Hidden along the forest floor
Were Fast-&-Furious and his mate
Who told of their regretful fate
They joined this herd all still intact

And found their story true to fact
They saw the stones, shaped like a heart
And at its base the covered part
Through weeds they went, and it was grand
A sprawling beauty of a land!

They lived there, not always in bliss
But with hard work, and sometimes risk
They made their way, and they did prosper
And strength of spirit they did foster
They taught their children of their tale,
How through careful study their herd prevailed
That when push has come to shove
When things endanger what you love
There is an answer we can find
First search the depths of heart and mind
Then check within and think it through
Alternatives are there for you.

Post Story Assignment

"When Push Comes To Shove…" Images That Speak A 1000 Words
For Each Of The Images: Write An Essay of (or Speak on) What Comes to Mind and
How The Image Might Relate To Something In Your Life. (Use Extra Pages If Needed).

1)

2)

Post Story Assignment *(Page 2 Continued)*
"When Push Comes To Shove…" Images That Speak A 1000 Words
For Each Of The Images: Write An Essay of (or Speak on) What Comes to Mind and How The Image Might Relate To Something In Your Life. (Use Extra Pages If Needed).

3)

4)

Post Story Assignment *(Page 3 Continued)*
"When Push Comes To Shove..." Images That Speak A 1000 Words
For Each Of The Images: Write An Essay of (or Speak on) What Comes to Mind and
How The Image Might Relate To Something In Your Life. (Use Extra Pages If Needed).

5)

6)

Post Story Assignment *(Page 4 Continued)*
"When Push Comes To Shove…" Images That Speak A 1000 Words
For Each Of The Images: Write An Essay of (or Speak on) What Comes to Mind and
How The Image Might Relate To Something In Your Life. (Use Extra Pages If Needed).

7)

8)

Post Story Assignment *(Page 5 Continued)*
"When Push Comes To Shove…" Images That Speak A 1000 Words
For Each Of The Images: Write An Essay of (or Speak on) What Comes to Mind and How The Image Might Relate To Something In Your Life. (Use Extra Pages If Needed).

9)

10)

Post Story Assignment

"When Push Comes To Shove..." Images That Speak A 1000 Words
For Each Of The Images: Write An Essay of (or Speak on) What Comes to Mind and
How The Image Might Relate To Something In Your Life. (Use Extra Pages If Needed).

1)

2)

There was plenty to drink and eat
And never was there too much heat,
Nor did it ever get too cold
So gardens filled and fruits shone bold.

But then... it came, misfortune struck!
The Valley Try... was drying up!
The sunshine shone relentlessly!

It was a striking sight to see,
Fields of green, soon turned to brown
And fruits, were no where to be found.

Post Story Assignment *(Page 2 Continued)*
"When Push Comes To Shove..." That Speak A 1000 Words
For Each Of The Images: Write An Essay of (or Speak on) What Comes to Mind and How The Image Might Relate To Something In Your Life. (Use Extra Pages If Needed).

3)

4)

Post Story Assignment *(Page 3 Continued)*
"When Push Comes To Shove..." Images That Speak A 1000 Words
For Each Of The Images: Write An Essay of (or Speak on) What Comes to Mind and How The Image Might Relate To Something In Your Life. (Use Extra Pages If Needed).

5)

6)

Post Story Assignment (Page 4 Continued)
"When Push Comes To Shove..." Images That Speak A 1000 Words
For Each Of The Images: Write An Essay of (or Speak on) What Comes to Mind and How The Image Might Relate To Something In Your Life. (Use Extra Pages If Needed).

7)

8)

Post Story Assignment *(Page 5 Continued)*
"When Push Comes To Shove…" Images That Speak A 1000 Words
For Each Of The Images: Write An Essay of (or Speak on) What Comes to Mind and How The Image Might Relate To Something In Your Life. (Use Extra Pages If Needed).

9)

10)

WHEN PUSH COMES TO SHOVE LEARNING FORMAT-I

1. Students are informed that with parental permission, they are about to become involved in a program that teaches learning and memory skills.

2. Students are placed into work group pairs in a classroom or area especially dedicated for this training.

3. Within the workgroup pairs, one student is designated as student A, the other as student B.

4. Taking each page one at a time, student A listens to a computer assisted voice over reading of the page and then repeats this reading to student B (who is kept from seeing the page in question). When students A has completed the reading of the page, they then ask student B to repeat back all of what they have just heard. Student A then rates student B (from 0 to 3) on the amount of recall student B is able to produce representing from 0, to approximately 1/3, 2/3 or 3/3-all, of what was read to them.

5. Student A and student B then switch roles and move on to the next page. This process continues through all 39 pages of the story.

6. Pair group memory scores are totaled and compared to a second reading through by the same pairs (smaller sub-sections of the story can be utilized to save time). It is expected that there will be improvement due to a practice effect, however the true aim of the exercise is to improve, through practice, overall vocabulary and attention skills, as well as memory. Teachers are encouraged to alter the implementation format in accord with the developmental level of their students (for example, smaller sub-sections of the reading by student A and the recall query asked of student B-within each page, can be used for less advanced students).

7. After three weeks of this training, once a day for approximately 1 hour, student scores on standard measures of achievement and performance can be compared scores on the same measures prior to implementation of the training to determine overall effects on academic performance.

WHEN PUSH COMES TO SHOVE LEARNING FORMAT-II

1. Metaphor hunt-Students are divided up into small groups and asked to come up with as many comparisons to real life from the story that they can determine. The group with the most comparisons is offered a prize.

2. Drama challenge-Students are divided up into small groups and tasked to act out or dramatize various portions of the story. In an auditorium or classroom setting, students perform each page of the story sequentially. The performance is video-taped and discussed and/or presented to younger students for interpretation.

4. Identification challenge-Students are asked to come up with something about themselves that they were reminded of from reading or hearing the story.

7. Artistic challenge-Students are asked to take one scene our image from the story and create an alternative following scene. Enlarged scenes or images from the story can be placed strategically in the classroom setting or home to remind students of certain adaptive principles useful in managing the academic or real life challenges they face.

8. Artistic challenge-Pairs of students are asked to volunteer to compete against one another (for a prize) performing the rap lyrics by the character *Careful-Serious* on page III, then the class votes on the winner (*we suggest here that some lesser prize be given to the runner up*). Then, the class can work together to piece together possible meanings behind the words in the rap lyrics. This is a fun way to invest the class in the lesson(s).

367 High Schools Student Ratings of When Push Comes To Shove

The following information is taken from the opinions of high school students regarding this book.

Note: the population utilized was 367 San Diego inner city high school students, grades nine through twelve, ages fourteen through eighteen, and roughly equally split between males and females.

1. Do you see the WHEN PUSH COMES TO SHOVE...story as an important tool to help students deal with the problems they face in school?

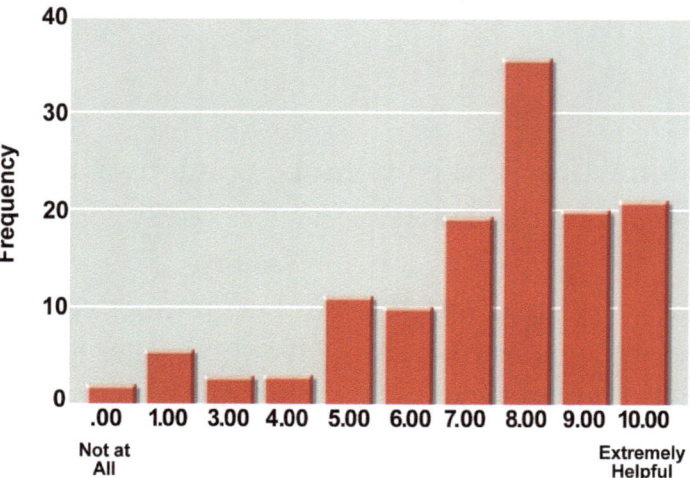

2. Was the overall presentation enjoyable?

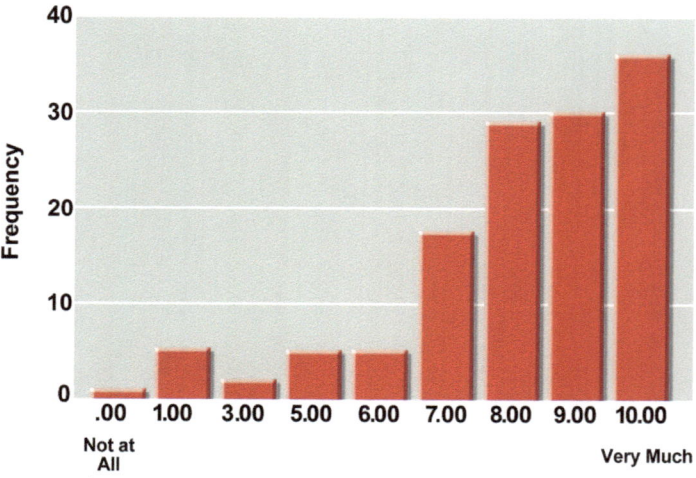

3. What is your impression of the overall benefit of the WHEN PUSH COMES TO SHOVE...story?

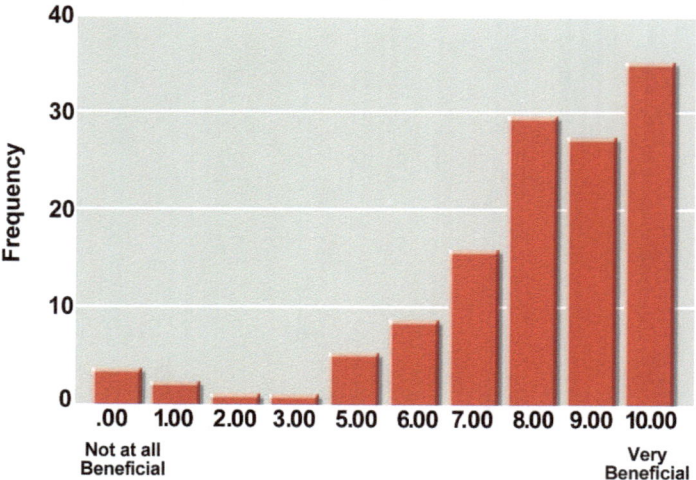

4. Would you like to see the *WHEN PUSH COMES TO SHOVE*...story used in schools across the country?

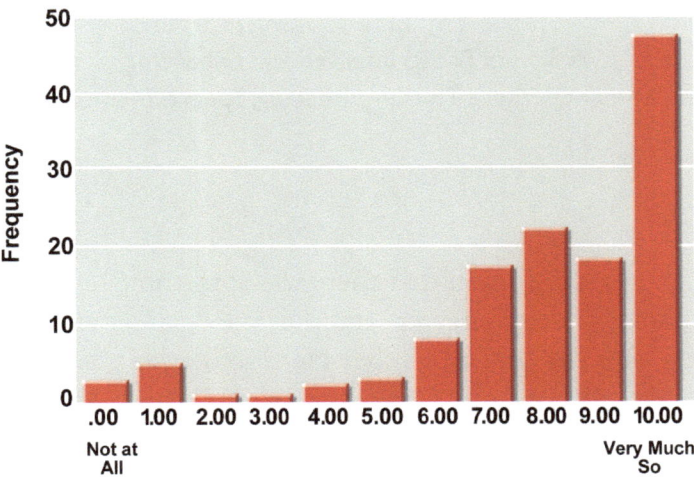

5. Do you believe that there would be important benefits to the education process from regular use of the *WHEN PUSH COMES TO SHOVE*...story?

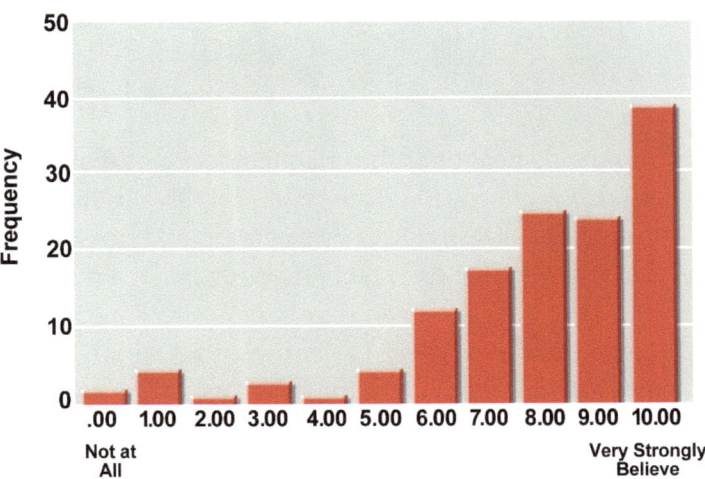

6. Do you believe that there could be important benefits in how children learn to deal with conflict at school from regular review of the *WHEN PUSH COMES TO SHOVE*...story?

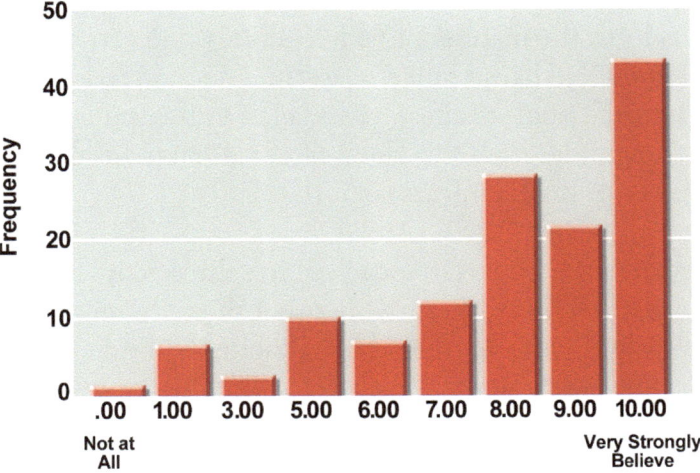

THEMATICAL TABLE OF CONTENTS FOR
WHEN PUSH COMES TO SHOVE (WPCTS)
Critical Thinking Training Program
A School Based Intervention Enhancing
Cognitive Development, Critical Thinking, Reading, Speech Memory and Vocabulary

CHAPTER 1

Page 1-This page addresses the notion that there was something definitive (*i.e. "most curious"*) about the names of the characters and that they had different perspectives or approaches to dealing with the challenges they faced in life (*i.e. "different theorist"*). What is a theory? This is a question that one can explore with young readers at this juncture.

Page 2-This page outlines the demeanor of the character Fast-and-Furious who is more or less a slave to his passions. He is overtly indulgent and impulsive in nature. He has very little frustration-tolerance often reacts excessively to provocation and he is known to be extremely adventurous. In fact, he is an unbridled risk taker and is always in a rush to do things.

Page 3-This page sets forth the character of Careful-Serious which is that of moving thoughtfully and diligently through the challenges he faces. The cornerstone of his personality is that he moves to expand the scope of his options and alternatives by gaining more information, through consultation, study, and reflection. Then, he chooses a direction based on what seems the most advantageous, given this wider field of choices now available to him.

Page 4-This page sets forth the manner of So Mysterious who can be characterized as somewhat timid in nature. He likes to take it easy and does not take well to moving in new directions. He tends to hold steadfast to his belief in the status quo. He tends to be rather fearful of anything other than the "tried and true" methods of solving problems. He is not one to venture out of his comfort zone.

Page 5-This page presents the notion that each of the three goat characters is a chief or leader of a herd of goats. This page establishes that the followers of each leader tend emulate the problem-solving style of their chief. Despite their differences, they all appeared to function adequately in the Valley Try, while the living was easy (i.e. the living in this situation was not particularly challenging).

CHAPTER 2

Page 6-This important page sets in motion the major dilemma of the story which confronts each of the leaders, the *drought of the Valley Try*. More or less it presents the notion that life often requires us to adapt to change. It also captures the idea of response to crises level changes. Crisis level change, while encompassing commonly acknowledged experiences among society (e.g. grief, great personal loss, etc.) also are very subjective in nature, depending to a great extent upon how the individual *translates* his or her experience. Nevertheless, this page is designed to serve as framework for responding to crises/change, not overly impulsively, not with avoidance, but in a balanced, informed, supportive and thoughtful way. It is generally useful then to move to and draw from real life examples of responding to change or crises.

Page 7-This page outlines the effort of the leaders to come together and determine a mutual course of action to deal with the crisis facing the entire population

Page 8-This page lays out the vague consensus of understanding amongst the leaders that there was purportedly some other place that exist (*The Valley of Alternative*) in which food and water were plentiful.

Page 9-This page illustrates how the leaders were not able come to terms on the best way to deal with the problem. Accordingly, each of the tribes took a different stance on how they chose to proceed.

Page 10-This page delineates how *Fast and Furious*, rushed on ahead with what he felt like would be the best way to meet his crews immediate need of thirst and hunger, without thinking of potential risks in his approach. He went forward without studying the problem in more depth *"Fast and Furious said "move out!", His herd charged on with cheers and shouts*, the WPCTS critical thinking training program creates an opportunity to address a certain response-style without confronting a person directly (*"…You see.. we do not easily fear, and our chance is better there than here"*)

CHAPTER 3

<u>Page 11</u>-This page lays out the proclamation by So-Mysterious that he and his *"crew"* were choosing to *"stay put"*. This was the choice he made for how his group would respond to the drought of *The Valley Try*. He makes the case to his group that they've always been able to rely on *The Valley Try* providing what was needed and that it was not necessary to make any changes. He, more or less says, "we need to stick only with what has always worked in the past"-if we are to have the best chance of coming out okay."

<u>Page 12</u>-This page illustrates the coping style of Careful-Serious and it shows him as one who seeks consultation with an elder concerning a difficult situation. The elder, however, refers him to a source of information that is greater than that which he possesses (*"The Sage of Trees"*). However, he gives the caveat that attaining access to this source was difficult and entailed great effort and perseverance. He indicates that it will be important to keep faith in his course of action, given the arduous nature of the effort required to gain access to this knowledge (i.e. If you allow the toughness of the endeavor to get to you it's… *"Access denied"* to wisdom needed for success.

<u>Page 13</u>-This page describes how the climb or "ascent" up the mountain to reach the renowned "Sage of Trees" was *indeed* exceptionally challenging. The steep angle of the climb, the cold winds and the clouds presented harsh and austere conditions that discouraged one from continuing upward. Discuss how this relates to life.

<u>Page 14</u>-This page introduces the notion of how, nonetheless the difficult conditions which "pressed" him greatly, *Careful-Serious* focused on moving forward one step at a time. Finally, he was encouraged by *"the tell-tail sign"* [here one can explore this idiom and relate it to other instances where one can be helped by observing a *tell-tail sign* (*e.g. if everyone is off the street where this is usually not the case, something bad may be about to happen*)] [or one can explore other idioms like "where there's smoke there's fire"]. Careful Serious' "tell-tail sign" that he was on the right track was. *"branches reaching for the sky, while at its base two holes like eyes"*. Also, as he got closer to *Sage of Trees*, the conditions around him changed from austere and cold, to warm and pleasant (*"the air warmed and then all around were singing birds with pretty sounds"*). This metaphor is likened to the notion of the "light at the end of the tunnel".

CHAPTER 3

Page 15-This page depicts *Careful-Serious*, who had finally attained his *hard-won interaction* with the *Sage-of-Trees*. *Careful Serious* was anxious to become *informed* about how he might best manage the situation faced by he and his herd, so he moved to engage the *Sage of Trees* (*"Great Sage-of-Trees, he did begin…"*) in a discussion on what he should do. Much to his chagrin, he is immediately, albeit somewhat rudely silenced (*"Hush-hush, its leaves retorted then"*) by the *Sage-of-Trees*. This highlights the notion that, however frustrating, often quiet patience, calm and marked attentiveness is a *prerequisite* for learning and understanding. Fortunately, *Careful-Serious* has the wherewithal to comply (*"He sat and quietly obeyed…"*).

Pages 16, 17, 18-As he sits listening to the *songs of the birds*, these songs suddenly become intelligible as lyrically expressed directions for traversing the perilous Valley-of-Alternative (i.e. some advice, that is initially hard to understand, may make sense later).

Page 19-This page describes how, *Careful-Serious* diligently *documents* all of the information he is given, by the *singing birds*. Such included things like paying attention to landmarks, as well as caveats and warnings about what he should do when, and how much time there is allotted to spend at various locations.

CHAPTER 4

Page 20-This scene switching page brings the audience or reader back to a focus on what is happening with the **Fast and Furious Crew.** Unfortunately, his crew lacked knowledge of the danger associated with the upside down "Y" tree landmark! The *singing bird's* advice to *Careful-Serious* was critical to survival! The *singing birds*, gave he and his crew *clarity* on how they should proceed in the situation.

Because *Fast-and-Furious* and his group were not privy to the understanding that the safety of their group, at this juncture, required traversing only through *the middle* of the *"Stone shaped like a Y, that's sitting rather upside down"*. The misfortunate ones whom, by happenstance, walked outside of this area were *captured* by giant Ogres.

<u>Page 21</u>-The scene on this page depicts the events on the previous page from the perspective of those of the *Fast and Furious* herd, (including *Fast and Furious* himself) who, again by chance alone, had walked in the *middle* of the *legendary* stone shaped like an upside-down "Y". Initially, they were unaware of what had happened to their comrades, but in fact befuddled as to how they seemed to have suddenly vanished. As they looked up further into the distance, they *saw with great sorrow*, the Ogres *stuffing* many of their crew in mighty sacks and carrying them away.

<u>Page 22</u>-The scene on this page tells of the *regrettable* fate of those captured by the Ogres. These misfortunate individuals were *consigned* to a life of slavery, grinding the Ogres meal from day to night on a mighty wheel. As if this were not bad enough, each morning would begin with the Ogres draining away the goat's milk, prior to beginning their day of hard work (i.e. their zest for life was drained away day by day). Discuss analogies to life in general.

CHAPTER 5

<u>Pages 23 and 24</u>-The scenes on these pages depict how *Fast and Furious* (and his crew), were stunned, hurt, and reeling from the Ogres capture of a large portion of those in their troop. He attempts to gather himself and rally those remaining to continue onward in their journey. He tells them that they must now call upon their greatest strength, *speed*, and move *even more quickly* in an effort to circumvent what has now become painfully clear is a place fraught with danger[("...*We must speed up our pace. I think this can improve our case! This Valley named Alternative is not an easy place to live! There are things that in the shadows lurk, but I've a plan that just might work! If we keep us moving fast, perhaps this tact will help us last!...*" (i.e. survive)].

Page 59

Pages 24, 25 and 26-The scenes on these pages outline how, in the effort to move more quickly through the forest, a few of the members of the group strayed from the path of the forest corridor (another area that was specified by the aforementioned direction-giving singing birds) and they became *"lost for all their days"* (i.e. analogies to following rules and direction abound here). Nevertheless, a crew of just nine members survived to reach a place called *"Luscious Lake"* (*Luscious Lake* is of course a metaphor for temptation and is a place that the *singing birds* had warned about. *Careful-Serious* was told not hang around that lake for very long). Again, not privy to this information, and being impulsive and indulgent in nature, *Fast and Furious* herd of only nine members, zealously rush over to *Luscious Lake* and gorge themselves on the succulent fruits available at this site.

Page 27, 28, 29-The scenes on these pages describe how all but two of the nine member troop (those two being *Fast and Furious* and his mate), having stuffed themselves to the brim, they fell asleep content and happy until suddenly, without warning, they were pounced upon by *The Wolves of Land Alternative* who *"With growls and snarls, and striking size... they caught the herd quite by surprise"*. The only survivors of this vicious attack turned out to be *Fast-and-Furious* and his mate. He and his mate because of their being awake and also due to the great *speed for which their herd was known*, were able to escape. The close of this scene finds the two lone troop survivors crying and holding each other hiding under the bushes.

CHAPTER 6

Pages 30, 31-At this point, the focus of the story switches back to *Careful-Serious* who is engaged in discussion with *So-Mysterious* about the merits of moving on to the *Valley of Alternative*, now that he has obtained a *fully-elaborated* plan on how they can proceed. *Careful-Serious* pleads with his fellow leader *So-Mysterious* to reconsider his decision to stay in the *Valley Try*. However, *So-Mysterious* is intransigent and refuses, holding up a list he'd contrived of all the things that *could go awry*.

Pages 32-Finally, *Careful-Serious* gives up this effort but strikes a bargain with *So-Mysterious* to, at least, let him take "the youngest two" from his troop to increase their combined chances of survival. *So-Mysterious* agrees. The *Careful-Serious* herd, along with the two youngest from the *So-Mysterious* group, then gathers their supplies and accoutrements and head out on their journey to the *Valley of Alternative*, following, "to the letter", the directions *Careful-Serious* had meticulously copied down when he was informed by the *"singing birds"*.

Pages 33, 34-The two scenes on these pages focus on the fate of the *So-Mysterious* herd that'd chosen to stay. Contrary to the *great speech* given by *So-Mysterious* on why it was *the right thing to do* (to stay); it did not work out well for this group. Eventually, the entire remaining *So-Mysterious* herd perishes from the press of the continued scarcity and heat of their beloved *Valley Try* ("*Herd So-Mysterious soon grew weak, At last they hadn't strength to speak, Then with the passing of the days, All turned to dust and blew away*"). Alas, the *So-Mysterious* herd just could not adapt to or accept the need for change.

CHAPTER 7

Pages 35, 36, 37-These scenes describes how *Careful-Serious* led his herd in the exact manner that the *singing birds* had indicated was required to successfully traverse the various pitfalls and perils that were inherent in making their journey, avoiding the *Ogres* and the *Wolves* they eventually arrived at the spot where *Fast and Furious* and his mate had been hiding out. After a joyous reunion, *Careful-Serious* welcomed *Fast and Furious* and his partner into their fully intact fold, explaining to them that they'd acquired clear-cut directions on how to reach their objective.

Page 38-This scene presents one of the most significant points in the work where Careful-Serious and his group, at long last, find the doorway to their objective, their new home in the Valley of Alternative. As the singing birds had described, this doorway "a stone shaped like a heart" had at its base an entryway covered by weeds and bushes. Getting to their new home, their place of happiness, required them work their way through said growth, and then to crawl through a small space at the base of this "stone shaped like a heart". This scene reflects difficult inner work it often takes to find our way to happiness. The path may run directly through our own "heart of stone" (i.e. for many reasons, we may feel we have to be hard-hearted to protect ourselves, but then it's tough to grow and reach a place of happiness). We must get through the weeds and bushes (i.e. we must reprocess past hurts and disappointments, and/or do forgiveness work.) to reach the so-called "promised land", wherein which prosperity lies. What inferences can be drawn to real life here? Notice how in the image the crew leader is guiding each crew member, one by one, through the weeds under the heart-shaped stone. What might this mean?

Page 39-The story concludes with the reformed composite unified group having arrived at their new home. They are immersed in the transition of building their new home. As they establish themselves in this new land, they are grateful and joyous to be there, especially after having worked so very hard to make it happen. The elders of this new group pass down to the young the lessons learned from their difficult journey. The pre-

dominant group that fared best in the overall scenario was comprised of those who hearts and minds were governed by reasoning, respect for one another, study, hard work, and perseverance.

This informs the reader/audience that as a general rule (i.e., "when push comes to shove"), we give ourselves the best chance to "live long and prosper" when we act to bridle (hold back) our inherent "fight or flight response" (a response-pattern that likely has some biological roots to it). At the same time, we are encouraged to push past what can become a far too familiar pattern (or deeply set and ingrained pattern) of avoiding addressing the difficult circumstances that we face. Somehow we must find the courage to face-up to (and step-up to) our difficulties. We can seek to become better-informed, and prepare to manage problems through counsel, study, and reflection. As this happens, we most often find hope for a path forward, when before there was none. Then, we can and must, move decisively toward our goal(s).

Epilogue:

In this work, each character's efforts to manage the threat to their survival represents, to a great extent, how we as individuals manage the threats to our own survival. However, it is important to note that this survival also extends to the survival of the ego, or the person's sense of worth and/or importance (see model below). Still, this work is limited in scope and primarily designed only to present practical guidelines and tools for working with people on some of the theoretical underpinnings of Adlerian Theory and related such works. Those interested delving more deeply into these concepts are encouraged to read the collected works Alfred Adler and related materials.

Self-Worth Diagram in Reference To Threats To The Survival of The Ego

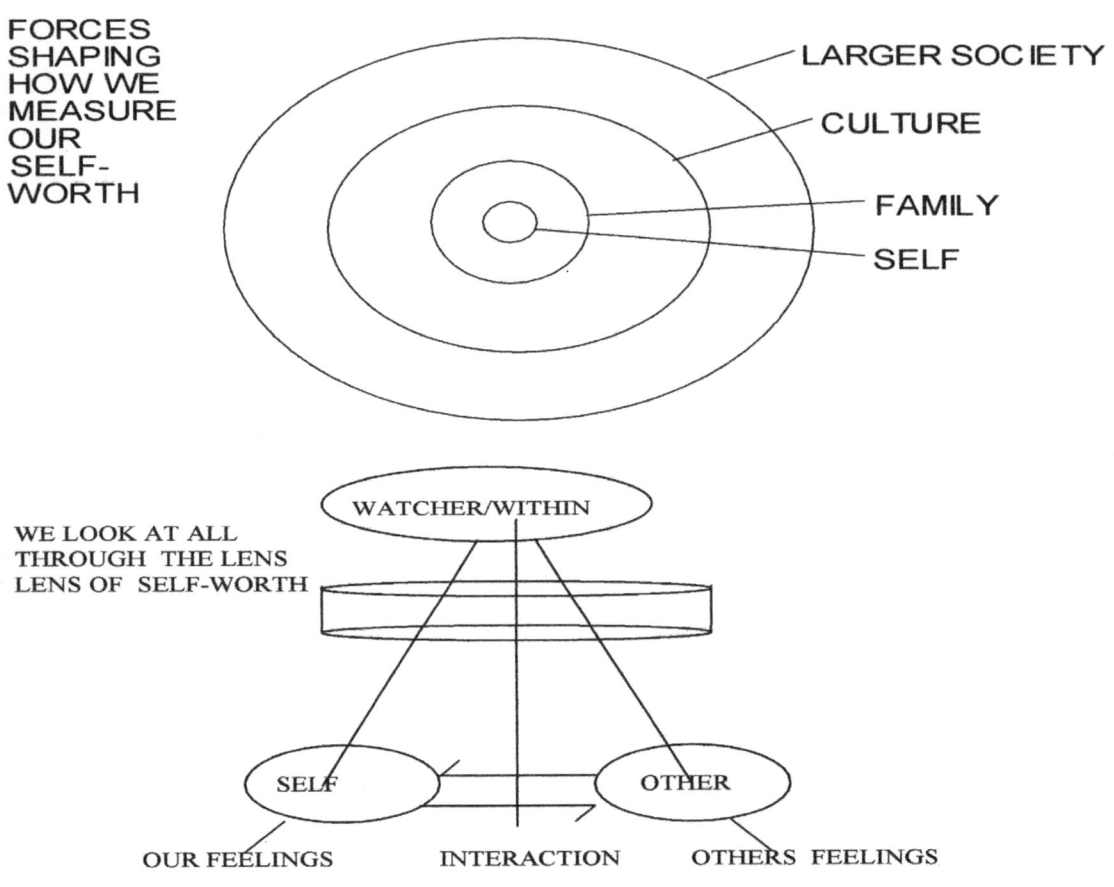

FORCES SHAPING HOW WE MEASURE OUR SELF-WORTH

- LARGER SOCIETY
- CULTURE
- FAMILY
- SELF

WE LOOK AT ALL THROUGH THE LENS LENS OF SELF-WORTH

OUR FEELINGS — INTERACTION — OTHERS FEELINGS

WRONG/MISGUIDED WAYS WE ARE TAUGHT TO MEASURE OUR SELF-WORTH/IMPORTANCE	VS.	THE TRUE AND ACTUAL BASIS OF OUR SELF-WORTH/IMPORTANCE
1. Seeking Approval of Others 2. Social Comparison (e.g. putting others down) 3. Group Affiliation 4. Riches 5. Appearance/Looks 6. Position/Job/Status/Education 7. Family Circumstance 8. Car Type Owned/Driven 9. Competance/Skill/Ability.		Self-Worth is an *inalienable* right all are granted at birth. We granted the following: 1. We are worthy of love/loveable. 2. We are worthy of respect 3. We are acceptable as human beings 4. Our ideas deserve consideration /regard

MAJOR PREMISE: THE HUMAN NEED TO FEEL *WORTHWHILE* OR *SELF-WORTH* IS THE DRIVING FORCE OF LIFE AND IT UNDERLIES *ALMOST ALL* ADJUSTMENT ISSUES!

An Example Of One Young Person's Narrative About The Work

M.B. 12 y/o AA ♀ // Foster Child

I compare myself to one of fast and furious's followers because I did not lead for myself I only followed the person that someone else told me to follow no matter what they did. Being a follower was not very great my life was just thrown around like everything else around me.

There was no thinking involved my so called leader was brainless just like this pencil lead. So therefore I was brainless to. I was confussed and mixed up because I was blinded from the life that my leader was giving me instead of the life I could of had.

Now I am careful serious my life is all placed together and now Im living the life in the slow lane not the fast.

Recommendations on
When Push Comes To Shove

St. Stephen's Cathedral Church of God in Christ Ministries

Bishop George D. McKinney, Ph.D., D.D.
George A. McKinney, Executive Pastor

July 15, 2009

To Whom It May Concern:

I am pleased to write this letter of support and endorsement on behalf of the 'When Push Comes to Shove' critical thinking training program, devised by Dr. Edward J. Murray III and his team at the Alafia Wellness center. It is clear that a great deal of thought and work has taken place around the development, design, and implementation protocols connected with this program. The metaphors and themes interwoven into the work have close parallels to the challenges and circumstances faced by our youth today.

However, I am particularly impressed with the approach outlined in the sample lesson plan for enhancing the reading comprehension and cognitive problem solving-skills for middle and high school level students. This, in as much as the only basic skills required to benefit from the program is for a student to have the ability to repeat what they have just heard read to them.

Many of the students in our community lag far behind these peers, yet most of the students at middle and high school level have at least this ability. Also, since the training entailed in the project is introduced and couched to students as *memory training*, it affords a later opportunity to make reference to the concepts and understanding around which the story is fashioned, after such has already been ingrained into their psyche. Also, this approach allows for an avenue around the emotional defenses that are very prevalent when it comes to counseling and advising youth at this stage of development. I am truly very excited about the prospects this work has for dramatically changing, not only how amenable students are to overall educational training in all areas, but for substantively ameliorating the lives and potential of the students. It is my understanding that he and his team Endeavor to prevail upon the president to have this work as a mandatory component of the education system of this country.

I wholeheartedly endorse this vision and pledge my support Dr. Murray in this innovative approach to improving the educational prospects of our youth. I am in agreement with the assertion of his team that were this to occur, it would indeed *transform* our country and perhaps our world in a favorable way. I want to take this opportunity to personally encourage *anyone* who is in a position to help Dr. Murray and his team achieve their goals either financially or in some other fashion, to please do so forthwith.

Sincerely,

Bishop George D. McKinney Ph. D., D.D.
Senior Pastor

"Upon this Rock I will build my Church."

MINISTRIES
Evangelism/Outreach • Bible Studies • Nurture Groups • Media • Social Services • Home Missions • Foreign

5825 Imperial Avenue • P.O. Box 740039 • San Diego, CA 92174 • TEL. (619) 262-2671 • FAX (619) 262-833

MS. ELNEDA SHANNON

Coordinator
San Diego Unified School District
HAROLD J. BALLARD PARENT CENTER
Parent, Student and Community Engagement
2375 Congress Street
San Diego, CA 92110 //Phone: 619-293-4431 // Fax: 619-293-4425
eshannon@sandi.net

11/27/2007

TO: Whom It May Concern

RE: *When Push Comes To Shove Book & Multimedia Production.*

FROM: Ms. Elneda Shannon

I am most pleased to offer my highest regards for the valuable and important contribution of the multimedia production *When Push Comes To Shove* recently created by a psychologist, Dr. Edward L. Murray III, with the Alafia Wellness Center, and supported by the San Diego Association of Black Psychologist.

As a parent myself, and in my capacity as coordinator of the Harold J. Ballard Parent Center, Parent, Student, and Community Engagement group, the quality of education of our children and youth in San Diego, is an issue very *near and dear* to my heart. Let me say without reservation that in my opinion, those of like mind should most definitely examine the many merits of this work and then make a serious effort help get this work incorporated into the curriculum at our schools, here in San Diego, California.

Certainly, this work represents one of the most promising, exciting and innovative approaches to enhancing critical thinking and problem-solving abilities in students that has emerged in a very long time. These abilities clearly underlie virtually *every facet* of learning in both the academic and social performance arenas of education. This is true for both the public and private school settings. I am very pleased as I anticipate the uplifting impact on education that will take place as this work takes hold in our school systems, first here in San Diego, California, and then across the nation. Through this work, teachers, counselors, and parents will have a very powerful and universally applicable tool for helping students move more effectively through the educational process. Few can argue against the notion that teachers, with powerful tools at their disposal, can and do lift up the nation!

Finally, I'd like to reiterate and agree with the crucial importance of the potential for enhanced *safety* at the school setting also mentioned by a number of other commentators on this work. I am most pleased to recommend that the *When Push Comes To Shove* production be included as a core part of the curriculum for our students at the secondary level. In closing, let me also offer that I look forward to the day when I might see this work done as a play by students in a performing arts class.

Sincerely,

Ms. Elneda Shannon

Carrol W. Waymon, President

San Diego Association of Black Psychologist Ψ
910 South 41st Street
San Diego, California 92113

November 7, 2007

TO: Dr. Edward L. Murray III, Ph.D.
Alafia Wellness Center
7439 Broadway Road
Lemon Grove, California 91945

RE: When Push Comes To Shove Book & Multimedia Presentation

The Association of Black Psychologists (ABPSI) is very excited about, and in full support of your proposal to get the When Push Comes To Shove book and multimedia presentation into the school curriculum here in San Diego, and across the nation. The developmental needs of our high school and middle students clamor for this work and it is greatly needed. Moreover in all my 40+ years of *weighing in* on the merit of various approaches to empowering African Americans in both San Diego and across this nation, this work is singularly important and unparalleled!

Getting this work into the schools is in perfect alignment with the mission of the Association of Black Psychologists: "the liberation of the African Mind, empowerment of the African Character, & illumination and enlivenment of the African Spirit". Getting this work into the schools is also not only a great safety issue, but an issue of independence and autonomy for all peoples of color, and the nation as a whole. The time is surely ripe for this work and I congratulate you and for not only the insight and inspiration of it, but the hard work that have obviously gone into the development of *When Push Comes To Shove*. This is a wonderful idea and I encourage all those in positions of influence to join us in a determined effort to bring it about, to make it happen.

ABPSI is in complete agreement with your analysis and projections of these benefits. After all, one of the reasons for the existence of the Association is that of addressing the needs of individuals and families around issues of mental health.

We look forward with great excitement to the unfolding of this venture. Be assured, ABPSI will do all it can within the scope of its resources, both physical and financial, to assist you in making this vision a reality: *When Push Comes To Shove* shall be interwoven in the school curriculum across the nation.

Please feel free to call upon the Association to make these resources available to you any time in your work with the show.

Sincerely,

Carrol W. Waymon

Carrol W. Waymon, Ph.D.
President, S.D. Chapter: ABPSI

SAN DIEGO UNIFIED SCHOOL DISTRICT

INVENTION AND DESIGN EDUCATIONAL ACADEMY
4191 Colts Way, San Diego, CA 92115
(619) 583-2502

Donald R. Mitchell
Principal, IDEA
dmitchell2@sandi.net

November 16, 2007

To Whom It May Concern:

Regarding "*When Push Comes To Shove*" production.

This recommendation is written about what may be the most extraordinary adjunct to the education process that I have encountered in all my many years of involvement in the education process. Our school was graced to have been one of the early targets of the multimedia production: **When Push Comes To Shove**.

At first glance, this multimedia semi-animated work may seem to be designed for very young children. As one delves deeper into the substance of the work, the vocabulary, metaphors, and underlying constructs inherent in the production are quite far-reaching and applicable to all ages.

This work invokes crucial understandings, while cultivating critical thinking and problem-solving skills that are particularly important to adjustment in life, and to the education process for middle-school and High-School students. My students took to the work "like a fish takes to water". I must say that I was filled with great joy as I witnessed how concisely this work was aligned with the educational and life challenges they face. The intense focus, attention, and seriousness my students demonstrated when this work was presented to them was quite rare, particularly for this age group. For me, this spoke volumes as to the need and importance of this work to the current education process. *Safety,* at middle-schools and high schools is a growing concern! I am strongly convinced that once established as part of the educational process, this work will do a great deal to foment a *safer* school environment, this due to the manner it tends to help students manage conflicts, as well as challenges.

As you can surmise, this work has my strong support. I offer my highest and unqualified recommendation that **When Push Comes To Shove** should become a *core element* of the education process for middle and high school students. I would like to add my voice to what will likely become a clamor to have this work as part of the school curriculum.

Should you need and further information please feel free to contact me at 619-583-2502.

Sincerely,

Donald R. Mitchell

BECOMING AMERICA'S BEST

Certificate of Special Congressional Recognition

Presented to

Dr. Edward L. Murray III
San Diego BAPAC Excellence Award

in recognition of outstanding and invaluable service to the community.

February 25, 2012
DATE

Bob Filner
MEMBER OF CONGRESS

Changing Lives Through Story Telling
Mostly Truth, Part Seuss, All Good

Photos by GREG CLEGHORNE

(L-r) Dr. Murray, JoAnn Osborne, Alafia WellnessCenter Mgr., Donald Mitchell, principal of Gompers H.S. and Troy Hilliard, 12th grader (mentored by Dr. Murray)

Dr. Murray speaking to students

GREG CLEGHORNE
Staff Writer

Dr. Edward L. Murray, Clinical Psychologist at San Diego's Alafia Wellness Center, – a consortium of clinical psychologists who help community members face and effectively deal with social challenges – spoke to dozens of students at Samuel Gompers High School Feb. 28, but not in the traditional adult-to-student manner.

Murray read his book, **"When Push Comes To Shove: A Tale Of Three Goats,"** *written in a style he calls, "Story-Poem."*

"The three characters are representative of aspects of the self," Murray said. "Each embodies a different personality which has to be managed. For example, Fast-&-Furious has to slow down, engage, step up and do the work necessary to address the problems he faces."

The students focused on his book and then paid close attention to the way he brought his characters to life with suitable theatrical gestures. Murray ran, jumped, hummed and engaged the students to compare his characters, 'Fast-&-Furious', 'Careful-Serious,' and "So-Mysterious" to themselves and with people they knew. Even the school faculty present read along and mused introspectively at Murray's work.

"I am very pleased Dr. Murray shared his book and positive life stories with our students," said Donald Mitchell, Samuel Gompers' Principal. "Our children need to know about the lessons in his books. Staying strong, doing the right thing and making good choices are to their benefit. Murray's stories share a great message."

A recurring theme in Murray's story is life's changes and how the characters deal with them. At the heart of the story is the lesson that while people both give and receive valuable information from each other, there's a source we need to

Student reading Dr. Murray's book

go to when that just isn't enough.

"What happens when a father loses his job," Murray said. "What do we do? Adapt positively? Do drugs? Act impulsively; sleep, slip into depression? Or do we get counsel, and work step by step to overcome? The process may be difficult, but it's something we need to do."

"As I say in the book, sometimes we need to speak with a wise man or learn from nature," Murray explained. "A wise man knows nature has answers."

Dr. Murray continues to enjoyed success developing culturally universal methods of interacting with many peoples. As a psychologist drawing on his cross-cultural experience using his story's metaphorical approach as an intervention tool he hopes people will get help when necessary, but will also look to their own insight.

"As I've grown as a therapist, I tell my patients to put a time aside to take a deep breath, let go of the issue, be still and something will guide you to what you need to do," Murray said. "Listen to your inner voice, to nature. Listen to your mind.

"When we do that, I say it's God we are listening to. If we adopt a place of peace, that's where God talks to us."

Murray said that among many techniques, this one is important for African Americans because of the level of pressures in African American communities today.

If Dr. Murray's books aren't on Oprah's Book List, they should be. Ms. Winfrey, Hook a Brother up!

For more information go to: http:www.alafiawellness.com

About The Author

Dr. Edward L. Murray

The author, Dr. Edward L. Murray III has worked for many years as a clinical psychologist in private practice and as clinical director of THE ALAFIA WELLNESS CENTER, in Lemon Grove (San Diego Metropolitan Area), California.

In his practice, he worked extensively with children and families, as well as with individuals and organizations. Dr. Murray began creating and using stories (such as **When Push Comes To Shove: A Tale of Three Goats Lives**), early in his career, when he was tasked to work with a large Native American population (The Colorado River Indian Tribes, in Parker Arizona) many of whom were not particularly responsive to traditional methods of psychotherapy.

Now story-telling methods form a core piece in a package of tools for mental health intervention. Dr. Murray was also board member and past Chairperson of the Children Having Children, Teen Pregnancy Prevention Program, an organization that fosters decision-making and problem solving skills in young people.

He has been, and is a central figure in organizing other nonprofits organizations geared toward uplifting the community. He was born in Ft Meade, Maryland to Melma Murray (a dedicated mother and accomplished artist & painter) and Edward Murray (a dedicated father, career military officer, and successful businessman).

As he grew up, he lived in many different parts of the country, as well as overseas. He believes these experiences helped him to cultivate an understanding of the ways human problems are similar across different cultures and circumstances. He was trained and still actively participates in martial arts (Judo; and took a silver medal in his division in the 1997 U.S. Judo Nationals) and he writes, plays, and sings music. He incorporates lessons from these areas in his professional work and his personal life. Judo, among other things, has taught him that one must *"get back up"* and try again, when life *"throws you to the ground"*.

Music has taught him of the inspiration that can be found when one works to be in harmony with life. Dr. Murray received his undergraduate degree from Indiana University (Bloomington, Indiana) and his masters and doctoral degrees (in clinical psychology) from Arizona State University (Tempe, Arizona). He served 14 years as an Officer in the Army Reserves, working primarily in the area of Patient Administration. From this he learned the importance of organization, routines, and record keeping. One of Dr. Murray's fervent hopes is that **When Push Comes To Shove: A Tale of Three Goats Lives** will offer many persons, especially youth, avenues for more effectively managing the challenges in their lives.

www.ingramcontent.com/pod-product-compliance
Lightning Source LLC
Chambersburg PA
CBHW060818090426

42738CB00002B/33